Leading the Way: Empowering Future Leaders for Organizational Success.

Nan McKay

Introduction

This eBook explores the critical factors that contribute to effective leadership development, employee engagement, and retention in the modern workplace. As organizations strive to cultivate the next generation of leaders, understanding the desires and expectations of millennials and Gen Z is most important to create the culture to attract and retain millennials and GenZ.

In this eBook, we delve into key statistics on turnover, retention, and employee engagement, and explore the four things that millennials and Gen Z value in company culture. Let's embark on a journey to create a thriving leadership pipeline and build a culture that attracts and retains top talent.

Table of Contents

Chapter 1: "Navigating the Talent Tides: Understanding Turnover, Retention Challenges, and their Impact"

Introduction: Welcome to "Navigating the Talent Tides: Understanding Turnover, Retention Challenges, and their Impact."

Employee turnover and retention is a crisis for many organizations today. If the tide does not turn, companies will flounder due to the churn of employees with 33% leaving within their first three months of employment and 17% leaving within one month.

Not only is the expense of retraining a potential budget breaker, the ability to produce goods and services with a reduced and untrained workforce increases the vulnerability of the business.

This eBook provides valuable insights into the state of turnover and retention in today's organizations. We will explore the profound impact of high turnover, examine key statistics related to employee retention challenges, and shed light on the significant financial and organizational implications that organizations face. Let's dive into the intricacies of this critical issue and discover strategies for mitigating turnover and fostering a culture of retention.

1.1: Understanding the Impact of High Turnover

The Ripple Effect: Unpacking the Consequences of High Turnover

Decreased Productivity and Efficiency: High turnover within an organization can have a detrimental impact on productivity and efficiency. When employees leave, it creates a void in knowledge, skills, and experience, resulting in decreased productivity levels across the organization. The loss of institutional knowledge and expertise can disrupt workflows and processes, leading to delays, errors, and a decline in overall operational efficiency.

Knowledge Gap and Learning Curve: When employees depart, new hires or existing team members need to fill the vacant positions. This transition period creates a knowledge gap as the new individuals learn the ropes and adapt to their roles. During this learning curve, productivity tends to dip as employees familiarize themselves with new responsibilities, procedures, and organizational dynamics.

This adjustment period can take a significant toll on overall productivity and efficiency.

Disrupted Team Dynamics: High turnover can disrupt team dynamics and collaboration. When a team member departs, it affects the team's cohesion, communication, and synergy. Existing team members may need to pick up additional workloads, which can lead to burnout and stress. The loss of a team member can also impact morale, as remaining employees may question their own job security or feel demotivated by the constant turnover.

Increased Training and Onboarding Time: Replacing employees who leave incurs additional time and resources for training and onboarding new hires. Existing employees or managers often need to invest their time to train and mentor newcomers, diverting their attention from core responsibilities. The longer it takes to onboard and train new employees, the longer it takes for them to reach peak productivity, further impacting overall efficiency.

Customer Impact: High turnover can have an indirect impact on customer satisfaction and loyalty. When turnover disrupts the continuity of service, it can result in inconsistent customer experiences. Customers may need to reestablish relationships with new representatives, potentially leading to frustration and a loss of trust in the organization's ability to deliver consistent quality.

Conclusion: The consequences of high turnover, such as decreased productivity and efficiency, highlight the importance of implementing strategies to address retention challenges. Organizations must focus on building a supportive culture, enhancing employee development opportunities, and strengthening leadership capabilities to foster employee engagement and reduce turnover. By taking proactive measures to mitigate the negative impacts of turnover, organizations can create a more productive, efficient, and resilient workforce.

1.2 Key Statistics on Employee Retention Challenges

Voluntary vs. Involuntary Turnover: Understanding the Different Factors Retaining employees is a critical challenge for organizations, and it is essential to differentiate between voluntary and involuntary turnover to address the underlying factors effectively. Voluntary turnover occurs when employees choose to leave the organization of their own accord, while involuntary turnover refers to employees being separated from their positions due to reasons beyond their control.

Factors Influencing Voluntary Turnover: Understanding the factors that contribute to voluntary turnover is crucial for organizations seeking to retain their top talent. Some common reasons for voluntary turnover include:

- Lack of career growth and development opportunities.
- Inadequate compensation and benefits.
- Poor work-life balance and high levels of stress.
- Dissatisfaction with organizational culture or leadership.
- Limited recognition and appreciation for contributions.
- A mismatch between employee values and organizational values.

Addressing Involuntary Turnover: While organizations have more control over voluntary turnover, involuntary turnover can also have significant implications. It is essential to examine the reasons behind involuntary turnover, such as:

- Poor performance or failure to meet job expectations.
- Organizational restructuring or downsizing.
- Changes in job roles or responsibilities.
- Misalignment between employee skills and job requirements.

Organizations should strive to minimize involuntary turnover by implementing effective performance management processes, providing clear expectations and feedback, and offering opportunities for skills development and growth.

Industry-specific Retention Challenges: Uncovering Trends and Patterns Different industries face unique challenges when it comes to employee retention. It is essential to analyze industry-specific trends and patterns to develop targeted retention strategies. Some examples of industry-specific challenges include:

- Technology Sector: High competition for skilled tech professionals, leading to increased turnover. Organizations must offer attractive compensation packages, stimulating work environments, and opportunities for continuous learning to retain talent.

- Healthcare Industry: High burnout rates among healthcare professionals due to demanding work schedules, stress, and emotional exhaustion. Organizations can focus on promoting work-life balance, implementing support systems, and fostering a culture of well-being.

- Retail and Hospitality: High turnover rates due to factors like seasonal employment, low wages, and limited career advancement opportunities. To address these challenges, organizations can invest in employee training, offer competitive compensation, and create clear pathways for career progression.

Impact of Generational Differences on Retention

Generational differences play a significant role in retention strategies as each generation has unique values, expectations, and priorities. Understanding these differences is crucial for creating an inclusive and engaging work environment.

- Millennials: This generation values career growth, learning opportunities, and work-life balance. Offering continuous development programs, flexible work

arrangements, and purposeful work can enhance
retention among millennials.

- Gen Z: The newest generation to enter the workforce,
  Gen Z employees seek meaningful work, diverse and
  inclusive environments, and opportunities for
  innovation. Organizations can attract and retain Gen Z
  talent by emphasizing social responsibility, fostering
  collaboration, and leveraging technology.
- Gen X and Baby Boomers: These generations often
  prioritize job stability, financial security, and work-life
  balance. Organizations can focus on offering
  competitive compensation and retirement benefits and
  providing avenues for work-life integration.

Conclusion: Understanding the factors behind voluntary and involuntary turnover, industry-specific challenges, and generational differences is crucial for developing effective retention strategies. Organizations must tailor their approaches to address the specific needs and motivations of their workforce. By implementing targeted retention initiatives, organizations can foster a culture that attracts, engages, and retains top talent across generations and industries.

1.3 The Cost of Turnover: Financial and Organizational Implications

Tangible Costs: Recruitment, Hiring, and Onboarding Expenses Turnover carries direct financial implications for organizations due to the expenses associated with recruiting, hiring, and onboarding new employees. These tangible costs include:

- **Recruitment Costs:** Organizations incur expenses related to job advertisements, recruitment agencies or platforms, and the time and effort invested by HR professionals to identify and attract potential candidates. These costs can vary depending on the recruitment methods utilized and the level of the position being filled.

- **Hiring Costs:** The hiring process involves conducting interviews, background checks, and reference verifications, all of which require time, resources, and sometimes the involvement of external professionals. Additionally, costs may arise from relocation assistance, signing bonuses, or other incentives offered to attract top talent.

- **Onboarding Costs:** Once a new employee is hired, organizations invest in their onboarding process, which includes orientation, training, and integration into the company culture. These expenses encompass materials, training programs, mentorship, and the time and effort of supervisors and colleagues involved in the onboarding process.

Intangible Costs: Cultural Disruption, Decreased Morale, and Reduced Engagement Beyond the direct financial costs, turnover also incurs intangible costs that can significantly impact the organizational climate and employee well-being. These include:

- **Cultural Disruption:** When employees leave, it can disrupt the company's culture, team dynamics, and interpersonal relationships. This disruption can lead to decreased collaboration, communication gaps, and a sense of instability within the organization. Rebuilding team cohesion and trust takes time and effort, and in the interim, productivity and engagement may suffer.

- **Decreased Morale and Engagement:** High turnover can have a negative impact on the morale and engagement of remaining employees. Frequent departures can create uncertainty, job insecurity, and increased workload for those who remain. This can lead to decreased job satisfaction, lower levels of engagement, and potentially higher turnover rates among remaining employees.

Quantifying the Total Cost of Turnover: A Holistic Approach To understand the true impact of turnover, organizations need to take a holistic approach to quantify the total cost. This includes considering both the tangible and intangible costs and analyzing the ripple effects across the organization. Factors to consider when quantifying the total cost of turnover include:

- **Productivity Loss:** The time it takes for a new employee to reach full productivity during the onboarding and learning curve period contributes to lost productivity. This can result in delayed projects, reduced efficiency, and missed business opportunities.

- **Training and Development Investment:** Organizations invest in employee development, including training programs and career progression opportunities. When employees leave, the investment made in their training and development is lost, requiring additional investments to onboard and train replacements.

- **Customer Impact:** High turnover can affect the quality of customer service, client relationships, and overall customer satisfaction. Customers may experience disruptions in their interactions with the organization, potentially leading to dissatisfaction and a negative impact on the company's reputation and revenue.

- **Organizational Knowledge and Innovation:** As employees leave, valuable institutional knowledge, expertise, and innovative ideas may be lost. This loss can hinder organizational learning, growth, and the ability to adapt to changing market demands.

Conclusion: Understanding the costs associated with turnover is essential for organizations to recognize the significance of retaining top talent. By considering both the tangible and intangible costs, organizations can develop strategies to minimize turnover, enhance employee engagement, and foster a positive and productive work environment. Implementing robust retention initiatives can ultimately result in cost savings, increased productivity, and a more stable and successful organization.

Chapter 2: Unveiling Employee Engagement Statistics

2.1 The Importance of Employee Engagement

Employee engagement is a crucial factor that directly impacts an organization's success. Engaged employees are deeply committed to their work, emotionally invested in the company's goals, and motivated to contribute their best efforts. Understanding the significance of employee engagement helps organizations recognize the value it brings and the need to foster a positive and engaging work environment.

Driving Employee Performance: Employee engagement has a direct correlation with individual performance. Engaged employees demonstrate higher levels of productivity, creativity, and innovation. They are more likely to go above and beyond their job requirements, taking initiative and delivering exceptional results. Engaged employees are also motivated to continuously improve their skills and contribute to the overall growth of the organization.

Enhancing Employee Satisfaction and Well-being: Engaged employees experience higher levels of job satisfaction, as they find their work meaningful, aligned with their values, and fulfilling. A positive work environment, supportive leadership, and opportunities for growth contribute to their overall well-being. Engaged employees are more likely to experience lower levels of stress and burnout, leading to improved mental and physical health.

Fostering a Positive Organizational Culture: Employee engagement plays a vital role in shaping the organizational culture. Engaged employees contribute to a positive and collaborative work environment, where trust, open communication, and teamwork thrive. A culture that promotes employee engagement fosters loyalty, commitment, and a sense of belonging, leading to higher retention rates and attracting top talent.

2.2 Surprising Employee Engagement Statistics

Disengaged Workforce: According to Gallup's State of the Global Workplace report, only a minority of employees worldwide are actively engaged in their work. In fact, the report reveals that 85% of employees are either not engaged or actively disengaged.

Impact of Remote Work: Remote work has become more prevalent in recent times, and it brings both opportunities and challenges for employee engagement. Studies indicate that remote employees may experience lower levels of engagement compared to their in-office counterparts. However, organizations that effectively manage remote work and prioritize employee well-being can maintain high engagement levels.

Generational Differences: Employee engagement levels can vary across different generations. Research shows that millennials tend to have lower engagement levels compared to other generations. However, Gen Z employees are emerging with higher expectations for meaningful work and a desire for purpose-driven organizations, which can positively influence engagement levels.

2.3 The Link between Engagement, Retention, and Organizational Performance

Impact on Retention: Employee engagement has a direct impact on employee retention rates. Engaged employees are more likely to feel satisfied and committed to their organization, reducing the likelihood of turnover. Organizations that prioritize employee engagement experience lower attrition rates, leading to cost savings associated with recruitment, training, and onboarding.

Organizational Performance: Engagement is strongly linked to organizational performance. Research shows that companies with highly engaged employees outperform their competitors in areas such as profitability, customer satisfaction, and employee retention. Engaged employees are more likely to deliver exceptional customer experiences, promote innovation, and contribute to overall business success.

Employee Advocacy: Engaged employees often become brand advocates, actively promoting their organization and its products or services. They are more likely to refer potential customers, attract top talent through positive word-of-mouth, and contribute to building a strong employer brand in the market.

Conclusion: Employee engagement is a critical driver of individual and organizational success. Understanding the importance of employee engagement, recognizing the surprising engagement statistics, and appreciating the link between engagement, retention, and organizational performance is essential for organizations seeking to create a thriving and high-performing work environment. By investing in initiatives that foster engagement, organizations can unlock the full potential of their employees, improve retention rates, and drive sustainable business growth.

Chapter 3: Millennials and Gen Z: What They Want from a Culture

Millennials and Gen Z make up a significant portion of the workforce, and understanding their preferences and values is essential for creating a culture that attracts, engages, and retains top talent. This chapter explores four key aspects that millennials and Gen Z seek in company culture: learning and development opportunities, work-life balance, purposeful work, and a collaborative and inclusive environment.

3.1 Learning and Development Opportunities

Fostering Continuous Growth and Skill Enhancement: Millennials and Gen Z value organizations that prioritize their personal and professional development. They seek ongoing learning opportunities and the chance to enhance their skills. Companies can foster continuous growth by providing access to training programs, workshops, conferences, and mentorship opportunities. Encouraging a growth mindset and supporting employees in acquiring new competencies aligns with their aspirations for advancement and career progression.

Embracing Technology and Blended Learning Approaches: Millennials and Gen Z have grown up in a digital era and are comfortable with technology. They appreciate organizations that leverage technology to deliver learning and development initiatives. Blended learning approaches, which combine online and offline training methods, resonate well with these generations. Offering e-learning platforms, webinars, virtual reality training, and other tech-enabled learning experiences helps engage and cater to their preferences for interactive and flexible learning.

3.2 Work-Life Balance

The Shift towards Flexible Work Arrangements: Work-life balance is highly valued by millennials and Gen Z. They prioritize flexibility in their work arrangements to accommodate personal commitments, hobbies, and interests. Organizations that offer flexible work schedules, remote work options, and the ability to maintain a healthy work-life integration tend to attract and retain these generations. Providing autonomy and trust in managing their time and output fosters their well-being and productivity.

Promoting Well-being and Mental Health Support: Millennials and Gen Z prioritize their well-being and mental health. They seek organizations that prioritize employee well-being by promoting a healthy work environment and providing mental health support. This includes initiatives such as wellness programs, mental health resources, stress management workshops, and fostering a culture that encourages open conversations about mental health. Organizations that invest in employee well-being see higher levels of engagement and productivity.

3.3 Purposeful Work

Aligning Company Values with Employee Values: Millennials and Gen Z seek alignment between their personal values and the values of the organizations they work for. They are motivated by a sense of purpose and want to contribute to a greater cause. Companies that clearly communicate their mission, values, and commitment to social responsibility attract these generations. Creating opportunities for employees to connect their work with a broader purpose can enhance their engagement and sense of fulfillment.

Making a Positive Impact on Society and the Environment: Millennials and Gen Z are passionate about making a positive impact on society and the environment. They seek employers who share this commitment. Organizations that demonstrate corporate social responsibility, sustainability practices, and community engagement initiatives resonate with these generations. Encouraging and supporting employee volunteerism and providing platforms for social impact can enhance their sense of purpose and loyalty.

3.4 Collaborative and Inclusive Environment

Encouraging Teamwork, Collaboration, and Diversity: Millennials and Gen Z value collaboration and diverse perspectives. They thrive in environments that encourage teamwork, cross-functional collaboration, and the exchange of ideas. Organizations that foster a culture of collaboration, establish effective communication channels, and promote diversity and inclusion initiatives are attractive to these generations. Embracing diversity in all its forms, including age, gender, ethnicity, and background, cultivates an inclusive culture where everyone feels valued.

Building a Culture of Belonging and Psychological Safety: Millennials and Gen Z seek an inclusive environment where they feel a sense of belonging and psychological safety. They value open communication, respect, and the ability to express their opinions without fear of judgment. Organizations that create a culture of psychological safety, where individuals can freely voice their ideas, ask questions, and challenge the status quo, foster innovation and engagement.

Conclusion: Understanding the desires of millennials and Gen Z in a company culture is crucial for organizations aiming to attract, engage, and retain these generations. By providing learning and development opportunities, prioritizing work-life balance, fostering purposeful work, and creating a collaborative and inclusive environment, organizations can create a culture that appeals to millennials and Gen Z. Building a culture that aligns with their values and aspirations will not only attract top talent but also enhance overall employee engagement, productivity, and organizational success.

Chapter 4: Strategies for Creating a Leadership Development Culture

Developing a leadership development culture is essential for organizations that aim to cultivate and nurture future leaders. This chapter explores four key strategies to create a culture that prioritizes leadership development: designing a tailored leadership development program, integrating learning and development into everyday work, cultivating a culture of feedback and mentorship, and empowering employees to take ownership of their growth.

4.1 Designing a Tailored Leadership Development Program

Identifying Leadership Competencies: To create an effective leadership development program, organizations need to identify the key competencies and skills required for their specific context and industry. This involves assessing the organization's strategic goals, identifying leadership gaps, and understanding the desired leadership qualities. Tailoring the program to address these specific needs ensures that the development initiatives align with the organization's objectives.

Structured Curriculum and Experiential Learning:

A well-designed leadership development program combines structured curriculum with experiential learning opportunities. It should include a mix of theoretical knowledge, practical skills development, case studies, simulations, and real-world projects. The program should provide participants with opportunities to apply their learnings in different contexts and receive feedback to enhance their growth.

Succession Planning and Leadership Pathways:

A comprehensive leadership development program should incorporate succession planning and leadership pathways. Identifying high-potential individuals and providing them with clear pathways for growth and advancement helps create a talent pipeline for leadership positions. Succession planning ensures a smooth transition and minimizes disruption when key leaders depart.

4.2 Integrating Learning and Development into Everyday Work

Job Rotations and Cross-functional Projects: Organizations can integrate learning and development into everyday work by providing employees with opportunities for job rotations and cross-functional projects. This exposes them to different roles, challenges, and perspectives, enabling them to develop a broader skill set and a holistic understanding of the organization.

Stretch Assignments and Challenging Projects: Assigning employees to stretch assignments and challenging projects allows them to push their boundaries, acquire new skills, and develop leadership capabilities. These opportunities provide hands-on experience, promote problem-solving skills, and foster innovation. Leaders should provide support and guidance while allowing individuals to take calculated risks and learn from their experiences.

4.3 Cultivating a Culture of Feedback and Mentorship

Ongoing Feedback and Performance Conversations: Creating a culture of feedback involves regular and constructive conversations about performance, growth, and development. Leaders should provide timely feedback to employees, acknowledging their strengths and providing guidance for improvement. This feedback loop helps individuals understand their development areas, fosters continuous improvement, and builds a culture of learning.

Formal and Informal Mentoring Programs: Implementing formal mentoring programs allows emerging leaders to be paired with experienced mentors who can guide, advise, and support their development. Additionally, organizations can encourage informal mentoring relationships to foster knowledge sharing, cross-generational collaboration, and personal growth. Mentorship programs provide a platform for learning, networking, and building relationships within the organization.

4.4 Empowering Employees to Take Ownership of Their Growth

Individual Development Plans: Empowering employees to take ownership of their growth involves creating individual development plans. These plans outline personal goals, identify areas for improvement, and establish actionable steps for development. Employees should be encouraged to take ownership of their learning journey, seek out development opportunities, and actively engage in self-directed learning.

Supportive Leadership and Autonomy: Leaders should create an environment that supports employee growth and provides autonomy in decision-making. Encouraging employees to take on new challenges, providing resources for learning, and offering opportunities for self-directed projects or initiatives empowers individuals to develop their leadership skills and take ownership of their growth.

Conclusion: As organizations navigate the ever-evolving landscape of talent management, it is crucial to prioritize leadership development, employee engagement, and retention. By understanding the factors that contribute to turnover, the importance of employee engagement, and the desires of millennials and Gen Z, organizations can create a culture that attracts, retains, and empowers top talent.

The Leader Accelerator Program, a pioneering initiative designed to transform organizations and cultivate future leaders, offers a comprehensive solution to address these challenges. Through a tailored approach, the program combines cutting-edge strategies, expert guidance, and practical tools to accelerate leadership development and drive organizational success.

With the Leader Accelerator Program, organizations can unlock the full potential of their employees, nurture a culture of engagement and growth, and establish a strong leadership pipeline. The program's holistic framework encompasses leadership competency identification, customized development plans, experiential learning opportunities, and ongoing support to create a transformative and sustainable leadership development culture.

By partnering with the Leader Accelerator Program, organizations gain access to a wealth of expertise, resources, and a network of like-minded professionals. The program offers personalized guidance in designing and implementing leadership development initiatives that align with organizational goals and cater to the unique needs of the workforce.

Together, let's embark on a journey of transformation and leadership excellence. Whether you are a small startup or a multinational corporation, the Leader Accelerator Program empowers organizations to build a talent-driven culture that attracts, develops, and retains exceptional leaders. Invest in your organization's future by cultivating a culture of leadership development with the Leader Accelerator Program.

Contact

Website:
https://nanmckayconnects.com/

Email:
nan@nanmckayconnects.com

Leader Accelerator Program:
https://NanMcKayConnects.com/LAP

Podcast Channel:
TrailBlazers Impact

YouTube Channel:
SignificanceAfter60

YouTube Channel:
TraliBlazers Impact Interviews

Instagram:
https://instagram.com/NanMcKayConnects

LinkedIn:
https://www.linkedin.com/company/NanMcKayConnects

Twitter:
https://www.twitter.com/NanMcKayConnect

Facebook:
https://www.facebook.com/NanMcKayConnects

www.ingramcontent.com/pod-product-compliance
Lightning Source LLC
Chambersburg PA
CBHW060850260726